Homecoming

(New & Selected Poems)

Dike Okoro

Cyberwit.net
HIG 45 Kaushambi Kunj, Kalindipuram
Allahabad - 211011 (U.P.) India
http://www.cyberwit.net
Tel: +(91) 9415091004 +(91) (532) 2552257
E-mail: info@cyberwit.net

Printed at Repro India Limited.

Acknowledgement

"Confirmation," "Lagos, Night" and "Don't forget" appeared in *Indiana Voice Journal*. "Homecoming" appeared in *Bolts of Silk*.

"Invictus," "Salvation" and "Again" appeared in *Ken*Again Magazine*.

"After Edwidge Danticat," "Rituals," "Fishing" & "Wordsmith" appeared in *The Caribbean Writer.*

"Tell it like it is" & "Metaphors for a Generation" appeared *Scarlet Leaf Review.*

"She" appeared in *Full of Crow Poetry*

"Instilling the faith in our way of life," appeared in *About Place Journal*

"Not an ordinary dream" appeared in *Fiyah Magazine*

"Father's song," appeared in *Rigorous Journal*

For grandma Titi,
In loving memory

Contents

Homecoming

Trees stalk me in sleep.
My silence is the dirge of
A river collecting shadows
Where the sun is a wanderer
And the lonely canoe
A wayfarer.

Incidents at the Shrine

Let's write to them letters offering caution,
The gods whose footprints delay our dreams
At the finish line each year we run along
With them the race of hope, seeking
Fulfilment from the trust in wings rusty
From lies and betrayal

Let's write to them with pardon, even
When our eyes trailing their actions
Are filled with dirt as they
Have their boasts while we endure
The torments of regrets

The scavenger birds return to earth
Their claws eager to grab and tear apart
Meat for the sacrificial ambrosia
Their wait time and dedication
To their itinerant ambition

They are gods after all
Rulers of the sky
Where dominion is the language
Of dreams, and renewal of pledges
The reason for living

Their shrines they've built with blood
And bones to celebrate from desecrating
Their deity is the monies they loot

To gab the truth and ascend the throne
Where justice is an axe long buried in a tree's bark

Let's write them letters offering caution,
The gods whose footprints delay our joy
The transporters of failures in flights
That aren't new but must be renewed
To reenergize their missions
Even when old habits have turned mortal
Rogue games in a shrine
Plush and luxurious with lust.

Nothing new

the fish avoiding the worm in the bait
knows a day would come
when the heart shall betray the eyes

the lion hunting and devouring hyenas
cubs, lives to witness the day the hyenas
shall use the lionesses' cubs for a feast

the goose swimming in the river occupied by
crocodiles sooner or later will become the happy
meal for a hungry crocodile

the bird that is alert and dodges stones,
has a date with fate when one pull from a sling
sends it down in a splash of blood!

Candy jar

A candy jar is a toddler's best friend
I know the story too well
and can dwell on endless hours
telling and retelling its plot.
How playing house leaves kids elated,
and why possessing a fondness for candies
helps them dismiss worries. The reality
is this: Innocence thrives
in the company of comfort, and
kids handed a candy jar
are averse to complaints.

Septuagenarian

—For Niyi Osundare

Today, songs come to us from the market-
Place because our days are no strangers
To waiting laughters, like the poet
Whose songs soften the minds of a hard lot
To summon the song-thirsty to pick from
Moments tender the pages of his
Love affair with life.

Mandela

You had us all fooled
When we decried your
Banishment to solitary confinement
And you wove a quilt of forgiveness
From a heart unsoiled by bitterness.

M. Kunene

From the battles of my heart
I resolve wars to acknowledge yours.
Zulu bard with a mind zestful like an ocean,
Out of your verse leap metaphors amiable.
The glow-carrying birds sung from Marrakech
To Africa's hinterland, where the elderly
Protected are stories for posterity, and
The present neglected a crucible of war.

Rotimi

—for a friend lost to gang violence in Chicago, USA.

I knew I had to cut my ties with hope
Watching you struggle, that night you
Breathed quietly as the oxygen mask
Clung to your face. I should have known
Then like I do now, that the smile that
Wouldn't break from your closed eyes
Was also a message, especially as I
Remember the movement of your hands
And imagine the handshake that never
Was to be, this morning a truck drove
Past my gate, and I accepted the goodbye
You never said summed up your pact
With eternal peace.

instilling the faith in our way of life

i hand my daughter the regular house telephone
when she crawls up to me crying, but she instead
reaches for my cell phone, her tender eyes
squinting even harder, her tiny baby
fingers touching and sliding like my big adult
fingers would when i am making a call. technology,
i often say, has gotten to our future generation
like a spell intended to spread something good.
looking at her, even when doubts wade in, i compose
a song i know will teach her how happy i am seeing her
do what i could only imagine doing,
those years when the house telephone would ring
and we would all run back to the kitchen, waiting on
father or mother to answer the caller.
how sad it makes me feel, knowing we were afraid of
father's spanking and ventured never to answer the
phone when it rang. today my daughter has tasted
the delicious juice of freedom from a new season,
and the thought of forgetting the privileges of the
present has not crossed her mind, not once, for she
still crawls up to me, reaching for my cellphone to take
her imaginary selfie and do her ritual touch and slide
to open colorful images impressing on her young mind
things i hope will enrich her mind as she grows
into the intelligent girl we all expect her to be.

Father's Song

A phonograph record I play without a gramophone
each day I sit on a bench facing
the lake behind my house.
I listen to the blowing breeze,
pretending i'm taking in a message;
in my heart photos of father speak
to me. His wide-open eyes
corridors of warnings. His hand holding
his ear, a rebuke my siblings and I have
imbibed. Like water rushed down the throat,
washing down a sumptuous meal. Only, we
worked hard to keep to his words. The army
general we call father, who delivers a slap
with one hand when we acted inappropriately, but
draws us close to remind us how tough love can be
with a warm hug.

Not an ordinary dream

Last night, I found myself
In a country of the ageless

We are history, we don't
Want nobody's history,

Read the street signs
People walked barefoot

Robots sold food and
Checked customers out

At the checkout counter
I looked at the payment screen but

Realized my eyelids were
Birds without tongues

When I awoke I felt
The urge to pray, but

Even prayer itself desired
A committed advocate,

Not one half-awake or
Selfish with the slogans

Of mass appeal – like
Charcoals burning in

Daylight were only
Quieted by water

So this is no ordinary
Dream, I said

Reclining in my chair,
Happy not to be answerable

To sleep's drugging
And mischief.

Confirmation

I carry with me
The sea and the sky
Wherever I go.

When strangers ask
Why I labor the flesh
To resist fresh mistakes,

I remind them
That we all
Belong to the earth

And must fetch
Hope from sunlight,
If we desire

Peace from
The sea
Within.

Don't forget

When you plant a tree
You preserve your father's lineage

When you protect a river
You honor your mother's sacrifice

When you break bread with kisses,
You forgive hisses

When you shield from the heart worries
You grow wiser from life lessons

Telling it like it is

Each day I celebrate a major
Achievement, I am trying to
Tell my failures
To move out of the way
So I can teach my tongue
How to belong to an endless song.

Remembering my absent grandpa

Cut the coconut with care
If you wish to enjoy
Its meat and water, he says

We did just that,
Setting the green, ball-shaped
Seed of a palm tree on the concrete,

Then, my older brother, scrubbing
Off beads of sweat like the fishermen
By the waterside

After cutting open a large fish,
Measured the spot for the strike
Like a pool player, body aligned, eyes

On the ball, aiming
For a good hit
But instead, it was

His machete that we expected
To execute
The splitting justice,

As the heat intensified
And loud arguments broke
From my brother's card-playing friends

Who, like me, have eyes set
On the plates waiting
For chunks of coconut flesh

While the aroma of mother's
Jollof rice traveled toward us
From the kitchen window

Metaphor for the Generation

Catch the blaze with your cellphones
Or with a flash from your cameras.
There's insanity that's unforgivable
In the act of violence,
The celebration of stupidity that
Makes the dimwit a hero.
Sit before a laptop, and
Surf the web for Sambisa Forest
And you'll find the mating of acrimony.
Troubled souls stealing freedom from others
To glorify misfortune
In history's books.
Boko Haram they're called,
But the sage knows they're far from rams
Offered as ambrosia for their beliefs.
The killing of the innocent
To atone for the wages of ambition.

Lagos night

For hours I stalked the sky's glows,
And since they pelted me with silence,
My heart wandered like the solo wind
On a deserted bridge.

Tonight, I'm dreaming

Monrovia is a mountain I'm climbing reluctantly.
Men walking on their heads trail me, their murmurs
Dirges compelling the skies to tears. How I got here
I do not know. I have colors shimmering in the sky
To remind me life is a pattern without consistency.
I have wondered how this day came to be but have
Accepted that truth is a guitar that imposes the will
To pull its strings on whomever it chooses.

So, tonight Monrovia is a mountain I'm climbing
Reluctantly. Yet I know the mutiny gathering
In the clouds is more than a mere mirror of yesterday's
Bleeding torso, where blood spill, not the thrill
Of brotherhood and sisterhood, crowded
Festivals. And because people live to forge
Alliances with forgiveness, I know now
Why pulling the guitar's string is not another
Comeuppance but a chance to make up
For lost times filled with ghosts' blues.

Dawn

The brushing wings of the afternoon breeze
Rub against my face and I begin to count
The names I don't know but know, to forget
And remember the days of childhood. Only
Gods can say that and get away, I hear myself
Say, not once but a thousand times, like
An auctioneer bidding his counting and waiting
On the right offer. The salt of aging, the secret
Of the waters. I know why the birds relocate
In winter to avoid nature's spell and propel
A homecoming celebration upon their return.
The facts aren't always what they seem. Like
A fluttering window that flatters the dreaming
Vagrant who must make it to the street corner
Before noon, to find a song soothing for the soft
Sun, if his stories in the dark must be worth a
Miracle's touch, or even a thing worth remembering.

Invictus

This night is long
It has been a long night

I have been walking
Making new songs from wrongs forgiven

Planting new seeds from harvest crushed
Burying old doubts with a bottle full of hope

This night is long
It has been a long night

I have been working
Tilling the field to make clear tomorrow's eyes

While gathering the sky's glow
In a bucket I call my heart

This night is long
It has been a long night

I have seen where the river flows
It is in the busy dream I carry

Again

I

Planting season
Time for reason

Uncover hope
From the waiting rope

Shake hands with
A prayer on your lip.

II

Revelation is a tea
Drink it safely

Surgeries are 50/50
When the emergency room

Is a jamboree of
Judgments shaky

III

Have you cleaned your house?
I hear rhythms

Rubbing on chance
To lead into ears

The possessions
Of a drumming chest

Salvation

I

Cast your net in the sea
It won't bring you

The corpse of a flea,
Nor will it present to you

The confession
Of time wasted.

II

Worries crushed over tea
Is a recipe for regaining confidence.

Tides rest after a redress
Convinces them of

The price of duress,
Like the sun's prayers

Answered by the moon's fingers
Over grass

Over trees.
I know the revelation.

To take it literally
Would be unwise.

The fire in the heart

I grew closer to you
By staying away from you,

Since distance works miracles
To revive hope after separation.

What
I detested about the moon,

I soon realized I cherished
In the sun. They say

The wayfarer's journey
Becomes a grueling experience

When the load he carries
Is not properly packed.

I have come to
Realize it wasn't the season

But the reason for your leaving,
Which haunts me with regrets

Each day I am in awe of how
I grew closer to you

By staying away
From you.

Wordsmith

—for Derek Walcott (1930-2017)

You have journeyed now to the land of the spirits
To add to paradise the radiance of your words,
The joy that grew out of worries
Till it transformed into a miracle worth studying,
Every bit of it a lesson and an obstinate addendum
To our complex heritage.
I see you now holding a pen and a book,
Riding a horse toward the sea of eternal bliss.
I see you now speaking to a crowd enchanted
By your narratives of the sea the fish the sky the birds the foods
And the boats.
I see you now singing from the bottomless reaches of
Melodies that make the unborn rock in their mothers' womb.
Star buried but still glowing in the sky,
Your hands were made for beautifying the face of the earth,
Stitching wounds where a rancor prowls,
And making the distressed feel lively like Marley saying,
"Got to have kaya now, for the rain is falling."
The rain that fondles the palm trees swaying
With the breath of the breezes
Like a camp fire stroking the night wind with unrestricted desires.
Wordsmith,
Your stories are numerous like the fruits and vegetables sold on tables
At the Castries Markets,
Where day and night converge in the eyes of the traders
And discovery and appetizers are the tourists' reward.
Today, the wind is calling and I hear its message in the airwaves

Today, the birds are singing and I hear their melody in the rain
Today, the rivers are mourning and I sense the grief in the current.
A parable has journeyed beyond the stars to the land of the spirits
And reserved in the memories of the living are the flaming paths
of Footprints.
Painter of life, go paint our lost and found worlds
In the paradise of the gone;
You whose verse is a room many enter to
Rock to Marley, sing of Gros Islet, Omeros's incubator,
& hug the island's views from picturesque words,
Embracing nature's wonder from the light turned
On by one man's romance with language
That is today an ambrosia for the heart.

After Edwidge Danticat

the word heritage is not a pseudonym
we all use when we look back
to remember how beautiful the sun is
it is the fried plantain and jollof rice we eat at a nigerian
foodhouse
it is the *soup jomou* we eat at lunch time on sundays in a haitian
creole restaurant
it is the jerk chicken with jerk sauce and steamed cabbage we eat
in kingston's grill house
it is the *mangu* you scoop with a spoon to remember its sauteed
red onions in santo domingo
so we know while the head is busy kissing the sky
like citedelle laferirre
sacred not because it is a fortress that hides from all eyes secrets
but because the past bears a burden brutal
like haitian history
and all its tears and joys
that comes home to find a resting place
in danticat's thoughts
how i loved reading *we are ugly but we are here*
not because it is balderdash, but
for all the romance with pains
that cures the mind of impurities
you take the little girl's voice
then her grandmother's
then you weave a memorial
not with sadness
but with a spirit of victory
victory in the telling that is in itself liberating
her story

our story
the human story
ayiti's pride
clothed by the nakedness of injustice
transformed by rebellion's curative
ah, so soothing, this remembering of our sorrows
and you are certainly right, edwidge
death is not the end
the people we bury are going off to live somewhere else
even as we the living continue their journeys
through witness accounts also watersheds
like Guinin's inquest
not entered at the behest
of syllogism fabricated

rituals

For years i've tried to be a nightingale,
hit a note funky as I dragged metaphors
across opulent Caribbean skies, to
turn tree whispers and misty scenery
into tropical jaw drawers and eye poppers.
But because peculiarity begets familiarity,
I left the nest one morning
to take on Derek Walcott's voice and
ferry across islands
salt soothed to nostalgia.
Like Braithwaite's akan driven lines,
breathing, pausing
like the boats laying silent in St Lucia
on a sunny day swimmers find their way
screaming, pushing waves away
before hibernating in the kitchen,
where Callaloo crab soup, and green figs
and salt fish
-unripe banana, peeled
-sauteed with garlic, onions, celery and peppers
drain cold from the mind,
giving assurance to body and spirit,
as the curtain pushed aside
invites sun, and
the clouds pushing away
turn day into night.

Fishing

today i will stand over this canoe and believe in my
net while thinking of jacques roumain, the historian
whose edifice empowered mothers from guinin's
legends, today i will stand gazing at the jagged rocks
and the water splashing on sand, thinking of aime
cesaire, tracer of footprints marking ancestral
pride and the potency of heritage, today i will think
of kamau braithwaite without walking the tight
rope of memory and enduring the stab wounds
still fresh, when imagining how often the elephant
ambushed by poachers rose and fell, each time
a machete hacked through thick skin measured
the sacredness of blood and the salt of survival,
today i will stand and look the sun in the face and
smile without shaking my head for walter rodney,
fire that couldn't be silenced by water, oasis favoring
the traveler in the desert, today i will stand and
speak of derek walcott who agreed the english language
is nobody's property, as time, like fabric quilted, brings
together all that makes sense in the end, today i stand
to speak of jamaica kincaid without taking from annie john
my first cousin anne's protest, until the cycle of violence
snatched her voice, that summer i am still learning to forget,
today i stand to speak of lorna goodison without thinking of
the bird relocated, yet craving the greenness of its first tree
and hoping the same river from which it washed its beak
and soothed its throat will not lose the purity of its essence.

ii

Poem to be read without a duct tape over the mouth

i was once invited to read
a poem in celebration of African history
& i took to the podium papers conveying
the chopped heads of martyrs
the limbs of heroes buried in unmarked graves
the rivers singing the bones and the blood of the poor
who died singing villages wiped out of existence
the ghosts of warriors who died that the children may live
the hearts of mothers who looked the nozzles of guns in the face
and spread apart their own legs to preserve
the virginity of their infant and adolescent daughters
   & murmurs erupted to stall my show of liberation
but the bonfire set by youth
arrested the moment with that which was crystal clear
i craned my neck and looked for traces of bravery
from faces covered in tears
not from sadness but from a dislike for oppression
elders in discomfort abandoned their seats
echoes ringing from a dissident eased the weight on my shoes
while government agents waved their blood-thirsty fists at me
"son, you chose the wrong occasion and place
to aim bullets at folks you know nothing about, didn't you?"
asked a cranky guest, but the urgency of my calling
lashed at the audience
re-echoing the thunder i brought with me
angry waves aiming for the shores of silence
where tyranny reigned and revolution is outlawed
   & at the end of my reading

people with warm hearts smiled to open doors once closed
and somewhere inside of me a voice spoke softly:
"prepare for the harvest ahead, for you've just sowed seeds
on fertile soil, but you'll need a seasoned hunter's craftiness
and the red eyes of nightjars to take back day from night.

Mississippi Joe

oracle of the delta they call him
amin and lumumba he calls his heroes
malcolm x he says taught him to be amerikan
but proud of his akan roots
heard his maternal grandma is haitian
his paternal grandma an ifa priestess
& there goes the full gist
& like his mama he is biloxi-born
bred to never run away from adversity
every fine woman he knows
has a child that calls him daddy
this brotha on a mission to meet God
when his bank account on earth runs dry
mississippi joe old mississippi joe
got a letter from antoine the other day
said a flood hit town & ever since
nobody knows where old mississippi joe
went fishing

Obieti

At Obieti they hold my queen captive, her royal beads
Scattered at the feet of a chauvinistic god. They serve
Her stale food and mud water for lunch, mock her
With starvation from night till daybreak. She to whom
We sang of our land's beauty now wanders naked, her
Face once a charm to behold the boast of foreigners
Professed to worshipping dollars and pounds. They
Drill and suck her blood daily, transport it as black
Gold to distant worlds where nobody knows the pain
Of loss and the riots in the silence of the violated.
Daily I cry like the allay cat on snowy nights
Dispossessed of a caretaker's warmth and the cuddle
That comes with trust. In my moments of silence
I cringe but know paradise isn't built in a day and
For this I forgive the wrongdoer and seek from
Hope the fortifying elation that arises from self-
Indulgence, and in my own quiet manner mock
Storms that have turned the homeland a camp
Of survivors staggering through moments holding
On to faltering prayers. Even the lion wounded
By its prey knows it fate isn't dictated by mistakes.
Our dear queen lies in the arms of orgy-thirsty
Guardians, her fate a price attractive like the appetite
For good food; but we brave a new front from blackouts
And refuse the lure to partake in the exodus, knowing
The renouncement of inalienable rights shall not make us
Sacrifices for gods indifferent to their choice of ambrosia.

Remembering

Upon my return home
I sought a grave, my mother's,
to turn away from things immaterial
and prepare my mind for the victuals
of remembrance. To live day to day
without questioning one's purpose in life
can be a careless avocation. Hence
I have always consulted silence, if only
to delve into matters awakening. This way
I can look someone concerned for my wellbeing
in the face and say: Worry not about me.
Memory is a cloth I wear.

Gathering

Spare the moment a smile
if yesterday walks into us
in the middle of a debate
to turn men going crazy
into elders suddenly wise.
Our foundations of the past
were set on trials that made
no champion of a first-time hunter.
Risk made the failure better with time,
so when next the mocked hunter
returns with a giant kill
much is spoken to venerate his skill.
These words I lift to the sky by speaking aloud
since I brought no drinks but knowledge
to show my generosity in kind.

Things mother told me

Never laugh at the man who wakes up
Homeless in a town full of friends.
Always watch the ground as you walk,
For talking can also be a form of entrapment.
Arm yourself with a forgiving heart, for
The grave beckons the heart heavy with grudge.

Port Harcourt (I)

This is where your heart lives, you say.
In this city you speak about things
As if your mind is an empty hole
That needs to be filled with things.
Things that speak about things. Whole, or
In bits. Like the mother hawking oranges,
Baby tied to her back asleep; her one
Hand wrestling tray unwilling to sit idle
On her head in a crowded street. You look,
But the day is an impartial map of
Things you gave up to be you. Like a groom
In search of the bride he abandoned.
Now that the cockerel has grown teeth
And gutters smelling of urine wake you up
To the fountain of childhood you left to
Unruly custodians.

Cousin Ebenezer

(*for* E. O. RIP)

We kicked football on sand
To make new friends each day
We played under the sun,
Dribbling in circles until we ran,
Poking fun to recognize humor
In times of nationwide terror.
You were four years older,
But my maturity left you to ponder
How nature's mystery worked
For some and blossomed
In me
To give new meaning to hope.
I learned from you
To be weary of juju
When you asked me to pray
After our weird uncle brought me
Lunch on a chilly
Afternoon, and the bond we shared
Sprung in me the undeterred
Nature of ways that made boys
Men in the face of uncertainties.
Today I sit here alone
And wonder how the years went by, gone
With your light that guided mine
Even onto this moment, teaching me
That the undiminished ties that bind
Bloodlines have no end.

On the Old Man's Face

Wrinkles are admissions of
A visitation. I only see
In them steps of a journey,
But my aging father says
Caution resides inside those
Messengers of time. Even
Goes further to tell me: look,
I bear them too; this gift
That's indiscriminate when
Finding a carrier, yet presents
To anyone attentive, a story
As old as sleep.

Old Woman

Such stories about her have been told.
The child's favorite: 'when a full moon
glues its face to the sky cheek,
bats, wings kissing air, eyes zeroing in on target,
count the hours to feed on moths.' The children
gathered round her each take the detail
of her smile, until they are told
what they know because they too have
been witnesses. Of grandmothers tying
to their own backs, their granddaughters'
children. Not because bloodlines are deep,
but because rites of passage are handed down
through actions.

She

I see her every Sunday
when the testimony queue
leads to the altar.
Her feet firmly planted
before the congregation;
her eyes inwardly holding
an expression of elation.
When she talks
Rwanda's pride and tears
echo in her stories, and
you imagine the nightmares
of escaping on canoe, baby
tucked under dress, to survive
genocidal attacks.
If war had a teeth, you could see
the scars of its bites on her face,
as she recites a continent's eulogy
from one country's tragedy. This
woman whose stories conjure
the smell of refugee camps, the
smiles of babies chuckling to
erase mothers' fears. Though
she's not yet at midlife's corridor,
she has witnessed crimes
as old as creation tales.

Proclamation

Inspired by sky-bound glows at night, I built a palace of retreat
From where I watch the cosmos charm the earth

Inspired by water and air and wind and fire, I store memory
In the agencies of my living, day and night, to preserve my being

Inspired by ants promising their colony fortresses of convocation
In storages hidden, I search soil and trees endlessly

Inspired by the sun whose story is always fiery and heat-razed, I collect
Healing potions from arrows of rains

Inspired by the mountain whose head is always the eagles'
hideout, I wait
For the plants crawling on boulders and stones, sending up lessons
to the sky

Inspired by the flutters entreating the eyes to specter like butter-
flies in the sun, I imagine silence the voice of the poem unborn.

Because I was thinking of you

I left a stone in a pond.

Patterns

Where rocks wait for me to pick them up,
I seek the sight of a dove to set free the mind.

And if I belong

Now that ageing has taught me to love stones without complaining,
I will think again before pointing a finger at the sun.

Now that childhood has humbled me with phases of compromise,
I will think again before positioning myself in the middle of indecisions.

There are friends and then there are friends who will be friends
sometimes.
There are dreams and then there are dreams that will be elusive
voluntarily.

I did not kill the rooster that deprived me of childhood initiation
when called upon to do the killing myself but was left fuming
when there was

nothing to kill. A lesson kept close to the heart is twice as impor-
tant as a friend treasured. A victory earned at the loss of an
irreplaceable gift is to a

desert an oasis found. Now that ageing has taught me to love
stones without complaining, I will think again before pointing a
finger at the sun.

Nostalgia

The Orashi River's tales resurrect memories of home songs
I smell the river's breath and long for the shores again,
The inroad to the water world of childhood at dawn
When fishermen reveling in stories of night's passing
Move their feet on canoe to revive hope under sunny skies.

The Orashi River's tales resurrect memories of home songs
And I must be alone in sacred meeting with my muse
As the blue sky stares at the birds flying groups, and I find again
Reason to surrender to the amazing wonder of the winged travelers.

It is your greatness that I recollect, Orashi River, emblem of lust
now a figment of rusty waste, where once upon a time many
depended in the act of swimming for leisure and the fisherman
composed stories from opportunity to take home fish

after hours of sweating and standing in the stifling heat.
The Orashi River's tales resurrect memories of home songs
I smell the river's breath and I from nostalgia the mark of
Beauty that enriches the mind with memories irreplaceable.

Lament before the sea

Tell me how often we have waited for morning's songs
here men talk with tongues heavy with pain
and the honor of a land is wrapped in blames

We have danced by the shores for too long,
longing for answers to find where we belong,
humbling ourselves after shame mocks our heritage

Why healing continues to evade our grasp
we may never know. But our songs of faith
continue to echo across lands, like the roosters'

crow welcoming dawn's arrival
where familiar footprints are sources of anger
and the refusal of flowers to grow the wrath of gods

Tell me how far we are from seeing the morning,
here where men talk with tongues heavy with pain
and the fate of a land is tied to the paddle lost at sea;

tell me how often we have waited for morning's songs,
here singers endure tiredness to pick apart charlatans
after the birthcry of the newborn echoes songs liberating

Knowledge

In the village my grandfather walks with a cane.
His slowed pace he says is the gift of life's reward,
Since it took him childhood, midlife and old age,
To agree limping in old age is a blessing.

Umlazi

Somewhere among your mountains
A collision awaits memory. I take
from the experience the liberty
of knowing, since the past
also births the present.

Umlazi: town in Durban, South Africa.

I go to the forest

Into the forest I go,
Spurred by the desire to take home

A harvest inspiring a rendezvous &
Celebration measuring excitement,

Like the squirrel scoffing at the foot of
The palm tree, a kernel its treasure.

In life there is a lesson to be learned, for
Every wait to claim a prize keeps alive a fire

Delighting the heart with a surfeit of opportunities.
Remember the fisherman betrayed by patience

While standing on his canoe from sunup till sunset?
His return the following day is more than a bargain

To tramp on chance and put to rest the weight of regret.
This, too, is part of the will foraging for satisfaction

In a forest, edging ever so closer to giving up, until
A celebration of achievement cements the focus of

Eyes and feet built for the endless search and dance,
Where survival incites revival to exalt moments.

Harvest

There is a sacred harvest
at noontide, where
flowers delighting in blooming,
keep steady while
birds taste from nectar
the sweet juice of dawn.

Kofi

The dance has come home
and we are no strangers to drums.
Our tales of the past, colorful
like the peacock's wings,
invites voices to this
evening the golden moon's
gathering. Texas housed
your dreams, measured
your steps & praised
your rhythms. You for whom
seasoned bards
from a rainbow nation
clapped in admiration
of your song. Forgive me
if I thought you Akpalu, or
wept when you praised Dunyo.
It is said that the fruit falls
not far from the tree. You speak
of the coming again to these shores,
but I sing again of reuniting
with the shores at home,
the signatures of ancestral pride.
Where upon each return
I turn to times past
to detect from routes familiar
nostalgia's treasures,
the way things we once cherished
used to be. Robber free nights
when children played hide and seek

and mothers harbored no fears
for the prowling ritualist.
Ewe bard, your verse edified
our celebrated heritage.
Traditions tending to the land's bruises
when the mind labors itself
for answers while accommodating
a conundrum. We have kept
record of the fate of vultures.
Today we crave
the leisure of adventures
enticing like Obudu's resort
and Ikogosi Springs,
where the mind takes
from moments
what one might need
to sing again,
the natural wonders of
a homeland ever-song thirsty!
The dance has come home
and, for tomorrow's sake,
we hoist flags for the moment
& take from the hour
dreams harvested
to answer home calls.

Father

Thirteen mounds spurned the sun
in your mother's backyard
before your arrival.
Today, I know why the elders say
your name unties knots
in the gathering of the brave.
This praise song is for you,
as you walk through the amazing
groves of old age.

Chicago dreams

I still hear the sirens
And it's all back to normal business,
Every day the sun returns to the sky
And the streets grow in crowds in Chicago &
The news headlines of the past night returns
More victims from gunshots and gang games
And my blood leaps like the Red Sea waiting
On the Israelites to cross before punishing Pharaoh's army.
I recognize the feeling and remember like
Frost that two roads diverged in a yellow wood,
No matter how often the smell of blood
Rushes those apprehensive to safety's corner.
Lagos taught me to trust in bridges
New York trained me to believe in dreams
In Chicago I learnt that the oasis in a desert is not hidden.
I have homes built in my hair strand by folks I do not know.
They tell me you are Ok when you are not really Ok,
And that worries early in life are revelations that your own stories
Belong to you and folks you will meet later in life.
I still hear the sirens, and
I have embraced the gospel of lessons with guarded guilt,
Forgiving myself each time I walk the streets at night
Telling myself the stars looking down on us
Are like the departed whose glow
Are prayers keeping us safe
From the madness of gunslingers.

Forgive me for reading this

"Corruption has killed more people than civil wars in Africa"
—PLO Lumumba

Since potential only makes sense to those that listen to advise only
After suffering a calamity, let these words heal like balm used for treat-
Ment of bruised skin. Take heed, you standing close to me but
watching at Arms' length. I speak from the well of knowledge deep
like the riddle of the Needle that allowed a camel a walk through its
eyes. The world is indeed Large, but remains the size of a newborn's fist.
We wrestle dreams from Birth till the last breath and forget living out
our days in fulfillment Of our destiny. It is our story the world over;
collective destiny is An illusion because many lusts after fame like the
sniffing dog Tracking a bone hid in a heap of trash and never finding
it. The Wise ones have taken to exile, not out of fear but to be at peace
With silence, guarding their tongues as they watch the foolish ones
Parade themselves in the arena of fame like soldiers returning
From war and declaring a victory song for battles they know was
Won in the imagination. Can there be a song without a lyric? Can
There be fortune where there was never sacrifice? Let those endowed
With wisdom tell us how water got inside the coconut, if only they
Claim to have full grasp of life and the patterns of human existence!